AS STRONG AS
A MOOSE

AS STRONG AS
A MOOSE

Wolfgang Mieder

Silhouettes by Elayne Sears

The New England Press, Inc.
Shelburne, Vermont

Library of Congress Catalog Card Number: 97-67978
ISBN 1-881535-24-X

Second printing, July 2001

For additional copies of this book or for a
catalog of our other titles, please write:

The New England Press
P.O. Box 575
Shelburne, VT 05482

or e-mail: nep@together.net

Visit us on the Web at www.nepress.com

Contents

Introduction

As Strong as a Moose: New England Expressions is meant to be a companion of sorts to the earlier volume of *Yankee Wisdom: New England Proverbs* (1989), which contains the traditional wisdom of about five hundred proverbs. This new gathering of New England folk speech is based on metaphors that are usually more notable for their imagery than their message or wisdom, conveyed in the form of proverbial expressions, proverbial exaggerations, and proverbial comparisons. Typical examples for these three proverbial subgenres are "To search for a mouse in a straw stack," "If brains were manure, you wouldn't have enough to grow grass out of your ears," and "It's been drier than a covered bridge." These colorful phrases have accompanied the ups and downs of daily life for generations of New Englanders.

It is customary to talk about New England and its people as a somewhat homogeneous region and culture. People from outside the region especially have a tendency to look at the six states of Connecticut, Maine, Massachusetts, New Hampshire, Rhode Island, and Vermont as a unified whole—the words "New England" conjure up the image of quaint small towns in a rural environment or perched on a rugged coastline. There are distinct differences behind some of the apparent similarities, however. The countryside gives way to suburbs and the highly industrialized urban centers of Boston, Hartford, and Manchester. The rocky coast of Maine contrasts sharply with the beaches of Cape Cod. The same could be said about the different taste of sweet maple syrup from Vermont and lobster from Maine or baked beans from Boston and apple pie from northern New England. There is also little social uniformity from region to region.

Nevertheless, despite the variety encompassed by New England's six states, there is something known as the Yankee character that combines all of these differences into a stereotypical whole. Much of this general image is based on old Puritan ethics, with the well-known virtues of integrity, perseverance, independence, honesty, frugality, self-reliance, diligence, and ingenuity blended with a good dose of common sense, dry humor, and a New England "accent," so to speak. To the careful observer there will be slight differences from state to state or even town to town, and of course also from one Yankee to another. The following joke tells it all: "To a European a Yankee is an American; to an American, a Yankee is a New Englander; to a New Englander, he is a Vermonter; to a Vermonter, he is someone who eats apple pie for breakfast; and to a Vermonter who eats apple pie for breakfast, a Yankee is someone who eats it with a knife." James Russell Lowell put it best when he described the Yankee as "a strange hybrid of contradictions."

Both the character and the contradictions can certainly be seen in the thousands of proverbial phrases that abound in this historically, culturally, and ethnically rich region of the country. There are, of course, many expressions in use that are ubiquitous to the entire United States and to other English speaking countries. The approximately five hundred texts assembled in this collection, however, were chosen to illustrate a particularly New England flavor. They were all located in regional written and oral sources, and many were found in the literary works of such renowned authors as Louisa May Alcott, Emily Dickinson, Ralph Waldo Emerson, Dorothy Canfield Fisher, Nathaniel Hawthorne, Henry Wadsworth Longfellow, Herman Melville, Rowland Evans Robinson, Harriet Beecher Stowe, Henry David Thoreau, Mark Twain, and others. Quite a few phrases were located in various almanacs, the mass media, and previous proverb collections. Most of the rest were overheard in present-day conversations, on the radio, or during normal verbal communication. Therefore, many of the proverbial utterances recorded in this book are still in common use today.

Even a cursory glance at the twenty-one chapters of this book will reveal the many faceted character of these Yankee expressions. While hardly a single text expresses any romantic or sentimental feeling—seemingly in keeping with the stereotypical view of the unemotional New Englander—there are plenty of them that contain a wry or satirical humor that borders on the ridiculous or unkind. Some phrases are replete with big-city snobbism and the obnoxiousness of new wealth, while others clearly delight in building their grotesque imagery on down-to-earth vocabulary that stretches from rustic farm life to human frailty and even apparent sexism. The Yankee depicted in these proverbial phrases is by no means a Puritan perfectionist, but rather a person with the positive and negative qualities that are part of human life everywhere.

Such chapter headings as "Fortune and Misfortune," "Difficulties and Frustrations," "Frugality and Poverty," and "Diligence and Laziness" reflect the contradictions of human existence in general, while the textual examples, with their unique metaphors, belong to a large degree to the New England region. The verbal images range from stone walls to woodsheds, from potatoes to clover, from cows to catamounts, from cheese to maple syrup, from woodchucks to seals, from skunks to oysters, from covered bridges to Salem witches, and from whales to apple trees. So much for homogeneity! Yet, the collection of these apparent dissimilarities makes up a recognizable composite.

New Englanders delight in colorful proverbial expressions and exaggerations. This small collection contains some especially telling examples in the individual chapters. Because proverbial comparisons of the structural form of "To sink like a millstone," "Hotter than hell's back-kitchen," and "As scarce as horse manure in a two-car garage" are especially abundant, three entire chapters have been dedicated to comparisons with *like*, *than*, and *as*. Other chapters include additional texts of this type to round out the picture. Proverbial comparisons are especially wide-spread in folk speech since they express in a figurative and often humorous or ironic way a fact or situation for which a mere adjective would be less poignant. Traditional folk speech prefers metaphorical language based on realistic aspects of everyday life to intellectual vocabulary. But do not fear—even students and professors in the intellectual havens of the renowned New England universities will readily use this formulaic language when it suits their expressive and emotive needs. Many a boring committee meeting or factual lecture can be spiced up with a bit of Yankee linguistic ingenuity.

From time to time it has been stated that, with modern industrialization and urbanization, these salty expressions will be driven out of currency. This does not appear to be the case at all. Quite the contrary, it can be observed that these proverbial phrases are very much needed to add some color and emotion to the routine of modern culture. In advertisements, cartoons, and the mass media of newspapers, magazines, radio, and television, these proverbial phrases appear with higher frequency than one might expect. The same is true for modern literature and oral communication. While this collection includes a few examples for which a short explanatory note seemed necessary, most of them are so obvious in their metaphor and meaning that they will be used effectively for generations to come. Expressions such as "To be six feet and seven axe handles" (Very tall person) or "She'll have to wear that dress from mill to meeting" (F r all occasions) will probably drop out over time, since their antiquated images already need explanation, but most Yankee expressions will survive, even as new ones that reflect old New England charm and Yankee wit are added.

To be like a pig in clover.

FORTUNE
— AND —
MISFORTUNE

To hitch one's wagon to a star.

If he fell into a well, he'd come up with
a gold watch and chain.

Happy as a clam at high tide.

To be born with a silver spoon
in one's mouth.

I have other fish to fry and their
tails to butter.

To put the saddle on the right horse.

She was born under a dark cloud.

Let's see how the cat jumps.

To get one's religion fixed.
[To attend church.]

As much chance as a snowball in hell.

To be an apple-pie order.

He really fired in the wrong
flock this time.

Worse than eating bread and milk out
of a jug with a knitting needle.

To be laid up for repairs.
[To recover from illness.]

His wishbone is stronger than
his backbone.

As happy as oysters.

To throw up Jonah.
[To be nauseated.]

To be a cock on his own dunghill.

It's no haying day.

As likely as water running uphill.

To feather one's nest.

It stands out like a blackberry
in a pan of milk.

To be like a pig in clover.

Happy as a skunk in a hen-roost.

You're the smartest thing since they
started slicing bread and putting
a wrapper round it.

To get the wrong pig by the tail.

To come within an ace of
making a fortune.

You may bet your last shirt button on it.

To be a jewel in a dunghill.

We are swinging on the same gate.
[We are agreeing.]

He's so sick that he'd have to get
well to die.

To be a big frog in a little puddle.

Popular as a skunk at a lawn-party.

To talk tomatoes off the vine.

SPEECH
AND
SILENCE

All your talk will not build a stone wall
or pay your taxes.

To say little but think the more.

His tongue goes like a mill.

To be still as if carved in marble.

You are barking up the wrong tree.

To chatter like a magpie.

He's digging his grave with his teeth.

She could talk the tin ear off
an iron dog.

To be mum as an oyster.

As silent as the shade of death.

She talked as though her tongue
was hung on a swivel and was
loose at both ends.

Not to get a word in edgeways.

To talk a living storm.
[To talk a lot.]

Freeze your tongue and give your
teeth a sleighride.

She shut up like a mousetrap.

To talk tomatoes off the vine.

He knows how to keep his
clam-shell shut.

He talks a lot but says nothing.

As speechless as cats in cloudy weather.

She talked the bark off a tree.

To talk the handle off the pump.

You are making more noise than a
flock of wild geese.

His pond has run out.
[He has finished talking.]

She has a tongue hung in the middle
and sharp on both ends.

To have one's mouth nailed up.

His tongue runs faster than a windmill.

To talk like a mouse with its tail
in the trap.
[Much and meaningless talk.]

Not even a team of Morgan horses
could make me talk.

As silent as a churchyard.

As mad as a wet hen.

ANGER
— AND —
ANIMOSITY

Angry enough to bite a shingle
nail in two.

To take someone out behind
the woodshed.

As mad as a wet hen.

To be right up-and-down like a cow's
tail in their dealings.

He's so angry he can't spit straight.

To be at loggerheads.

To go at it hammer and tongs.
[To quarrel.]

She has no more use for him than a
sitting hen has for a midwife.

Meaner than a wild horse with
a toothache.

As unlike as a cabbage is to a rose.

There isn't any use to get up on your
ear about it.
[To get violently angry.]

To be cross as a badger.

He thinks he's some pumpkins.
[Of some consequence.]

As subtle as a brick through
a glass window.

To handle someone without mittens.

She gave him a combing out.
[She scolded him.]

I'll hit you so hard you'll starve
to death bouncing.

As mad as a bear with his tail shot off.

You're so green the cows will eat you
if you don't watch out.

To get one's back up.
[To get enraged.]

So mean he'd steal a fly from
a blind spider.

Madder than snakes in haying.

To like something like the devil
likes holy water.

As fierce as a catamount.

You're so low you'd have to stand on
stilts to scratch a snake's back.

You ought to tend to your
own knitting.
[Mind your own business.]

Accommodating as a hog on ice.
[Extremely disagreeable.]

As mad as a hornet.

He's small potatoes and few
on the hill.

You can't get to windward of him.
[To gain an advantage over someone.]

His soul is so small it would rattle
around in a flea's bladder like a pea
in a hog's head.

Like a cow chasing a hare.

INUTILITY
AND
REDUNDANCY

To throw snowballs into hell to
put out the fire.

Not worth a fly wing.

Of no more use than a spare pump
in a corn crib.

To look for eggs in a mare's nest.

Like a cow chasing a hare.

This isn't worth the north wind in
a rabbit's track.

Handy as a hog with a fiddle.

Doesn't amount to a pinch of bug dust.

Trying to fit a square peg into
a round hole.

To save at the spigot and lose
at the bunghole.

As useless as a screen door
on a submarine.

You don't need that any more than you
need fire in your shoes.

To throw water on a drowned rat.

He has no more business there than a
powder-house in hell.

As dead as hay.

To search for a mouse in a straw stack.

To lock the barn door after the
horse is stolen.

As handy as a sow with a musket.

As useless as a fork in a bowl of soup.

You don't need it any more than you
need a pocket in your undershirt.

That doesn't cut any cheese.
[Has no weight.]

To feel like a fifth calf.

We don't need that any more than
a frog needs sideburns.

Doesn't amount to a hill of beans
in windy weather.

You might as well be talking to a post.

As useless as a chimney in summer.

He is not worth the powder to blow
him up with.

As worthless as a milk bucket
under a bull.

To start in the middle and
end at both ends.
[To get nowhere.]

You don't need that any more than to
stand on your head in a mud puddle.

She doesn't need that any more than
a toad needs a watch.

As little use for that thing as a wagon
has for a fifth wheel.

It doesn't make a straw's difference.

He doesn't need it any more than
a pig needs a wallet.

EXCITEMENT
AND
EMOTIONS

To dance like a bird on an apple-tree
limb in spring time.

As lively as a chipmunk on a wall.

She is so excited she has to walk
sideways to keep from flying.

To go the whole hog.

He went off half-cocked.

As happy as a bumblebee in
a field of clover.

To be three sheets to the wind.
[To be intoxicated.]

Jumped around like a frog in
a butter churn.

He wants the whole world and a potato
patch on the other side.

As crazy as a fly in a drum.

Off she went like a trout with a
fish-hook in its mouth.

As full of fun as a kitten.

To act as if one had been brought
up in a barn.

She danced around like a spring colt
just let out to grass.

His head is swelled as big
as a pumpkin.

As chipper as a squirrel in
the fall time.

He's sorry from his boots up.

To be tight as a mink.
[To be drunk.]

As full of flattery as an egg is full of
white and yolk both.

He went off like a firecracker on the
Fourth of July.

To bounce up like a hare from under
the cabbage leaf.

To be right up on one's bean-water.
[To feel very lively.]

She flies around like a parched pea
in a hot skillet.

As merry as crickets.

He wants the world fenced in and
a slice off the moon.

As smart as a steel trap.
[Alert.]

To be as spruce as a bluejay.

She is as sour as a crabapple.

As lonely as a scarecrow in a field
of stubble.

Full of ideas as a dog is full of fleas.

To be stewed to the gills.
[To be intoxicated.]

Excited as a cat at a mouse-show.

Act like a cat in a gale of wind.

SPEED
— AND —
RETARDATION

Slower than the hind wheels of time
greased with cold molasses.

In two shakes of a lamb's tail.

He's too slow to catch a cold.

To put the licks in.
[To go very fast.]

Slow as a barge on a reef.

She is slower than the growth
of grindstone.

Fast as small-town gossip.

To be always on the hind
end of nothing.

As quick as a hopping grasshopper with
his tail on fire.

Act like a cat in a gale of wind.
[Move briskly.]

Slower than cold molasses
running up hill.

To be quicker than chain lightning.
[Very quick.]

To run like a Salem witch.

Disappeared as fast as a gallon of
ice-cream at a kids' party.

So slow that he'll rot in his tracks.

About as fast as a crippled caterpillar.

To be fast as greased lightning.

She moves so slowly that you can
watch the snails whiz by.

I've run the leeward this year.
[To run behind.]

Quicker than you can take
off a wet shirt.

As slow as the seven-year itch.

They rushed around like a whirlwind.

He ran as swift as pudding
would creep.

To always be late in the tide.

She moves about as fast as
a stone locomotive.

Slower than a hop of a toad in hot tar.

He's always behind like an old cow's tail.

Slow as a hog on ice with its
tail frozen in.

Mill around like a herd of cows.

COMPARISONS
WITH
LIKE

The dress fits like a duck's foot
in the mud.

Mill around like a herd of cows.

To stare like a wildcat.

Jump around like a flea in a mitten.

Cut off like a worm in the ground.

To strut about like a turkey cock.

Cling like a wet kitten to a hot brick.

To stand like an ass between two
bales of hay.

He looks like he's been hit in the face
with a wet squirrel.

To squeak and grunt just like a litter
of hungry pigs.

They act like a hen on a hot griddle.

This fits like a bearskin on
a woodchuck.

He has a voice like a foghorn.

To stick like a puppy to a bone.

I feel like a skunk in hell with
his back broken.

Sweating like a man mowing.

He looked like something the dog
dragged in and the cat wouldn't eat.

To sink like a millstone.

To act like a turkey and think
like a groundhog.

She jumped like a cat out
of a woodbox.

He stumbled around like a blind horse
in a pumpkin patch.

To loom up like a skunk in a fog.

This fits like a saddle on a cow.

To jump like a pea on a hot griddle.

He poured out money like water.

To look like a scarecrow.

It will go like dew before the sun.

To squeak like a sled runner on
a frosty morning.

To bear something like a lamb.

She waddles like a hurried duck.

39

Like a pig's tail—going all day and nothing done at night.

To look like a shirt on a beanpole. [Bad fit.]

I am sweating like a pitcher with ice-water in it.

To spring up like mushrooms.

To stick like a leech.

She has eyes like two balls of fire.

He slept like a woodchuck.

She's as dainty as a cow with snowshoes on.

BODIES
AND
APPEARANCES

His face looked just like a frost-bitten apple when it is beginning to thaw out.

As fat as a seal.

To look as if one had been drawn through a knot-hole.

Homely as a stump fence built in the dark.

As erect as a flagstaff.

To have a fish and potato face.

She wasn't behind the door when
beauty was given out.

As ugly as a skinned horse.

He is so thin he can drink a glass
of tomato juice and look like
a thermometer.

So ugly the flies won't light
on her face.

Homely enough to stop a train.

She is as beautiful as a picture.

To look like something the cat has
brought in after dragging it over the
stone wall and through the wet grass.

As handsome as a prize heifer.

He's as bald as an egg.

As slender as a reed.

Homely enough to sour milk.

So ugly that when he lies on the beach
the tide won't come in.

She's as dainty as a cow with
snowshoes on.

To stand up as stiff as a poker.

Her face looked as if she had been fed
on crab-apples for a whole month.

She is pale as dishwater.

Ugly enough to make a freight train
take a dirt road.

Breasts like raspberry popovers.

He has a head as round as an apple tree.

To look as though one were dead and
had been dug up again.

With hair like threads of gold.

She is so skinny she could swallow a
prune and look pregnant.

A figure like an hourglass.

To have a face that only a mother could love.

Beautiful as a flower in a seed catalog.

Contrary as a mule in a mud-puddle.

DIFFICULTIES
AND
FRUSTRATIONS

We are half way between the devil
and a red pig.
[In a dangerous position.]

As hard as pushing a noodle
through a keyhole.

To butt one's head against a stone wall.

She is bound to kick over the traces
every time she gets a chance.

That's like hauling a hog out
of a scalding tub.

We are in the right church but in
the wrong pew.

To get took down a peg.
[To be humiliated.]

You might as well try to hold a greased
eel as a live Connecticut Yankee.

Let's not make a mountain out
of a mouse.

He's been through the mill.

The house looks as though the devil had
an auction and left everything there.

You have the wrong pig by the tail.

Between hawk and buzzard.
[To be in a dilemma.]

To have to eat the cabbage one spits in.

That's like waving a red flag at a bull.

She collapsed like a wet dish-cloth.

To hold the hot end of the stick and the
short end of the rope.

He feels like a three cent piece with
a hole in it.

To have one's fat in the fire.
[Being frustrated.]

It was like finding the pebble
in the brook.

He butted in like a billy goat.

To be like a rat in trouble.

It's no use sitting here as still as two
rotten stumps in a fog.

To avoid the snare and fall into the pit.

Contrary as a mule in a mud-puddle.

He can either outlive this problem or he
can die and get away from it.

Not to find hide nor hair of someone.

A wagonload of postholes.
[Nothing.]

Let us show you how to tell a
woodchuck from a skunk.

She was up a creek without a paddle.

To gaze at the stars and fall
into the ditch.

He must have been brought up
in a saw mill.
[Ill-mannered.]

To swallow the cow and get stuck
on the tail.

He's so miserly that he crawls under the door to save the hinges.

FRUGALITY
AND
POVERTY

He is as tight as last winter's long johns.

She makes pancakes so thin they
have but one side.

As poor as a fence rail.

This is way up in the picture.
[Too expensive.]

He is so miserly that he crawls under
the door to save the hinges.

To make the strap and the buckle meet.

As poor as poverty in a gale of wind.

She'd skin a woodchuck to save a cent.

To have pretty hard sledding.
[Hard times.]

Frugal as a poor farmer's wife.

He is so tight, his eyelids squeak
when he winks.

As snug as the skin of your teeth.
[Miserly.]

To be as poor as a church mouse.

He's so tight he'd skin a flea for
the hide and taller.

You are so stingy you would take
candy from a child.

To have neither horn nor hoof.
[To be poor.]

Poor as watermelon rinds.

As empty as a New England purse.

His land looks as poor as poverty.

She'll have to wear that dress from
mill to meeting.
[For all occasions.]

As tight as the paper on the wall.

He is so cheap he'd steal a penny off
a dead man's eyes.

To be as poor as a skin-milk cheese.

They are trying to keep the wolf
from the door.

As poor as the shadow of a bean pole.

She's so tight she would pinch the dollar
till the eagle screams.

To pay one's creditors with a
flying fore-topsail.
[To run away from one's debts.]

As pretty as a goggle-eyed perch.

LOVE
— AND —
KISSES

Lips like a bunch of ripe strawberries.

She is pretty enough to take
to a barn dance.

As merry as a marriage bell.

That kiss sounded like a cow pulling her
foot out of the mud.

To set oneself up in a butter tub.
[To marry a wealthy woman.]

To submit to petticoat government.

To be as cute as a bug's ear.

She wasn't a girl to let her heart run
away with her head.

As hopeful as an old maid looking
under the bed.

Red as a girl's lips.

We are running in double harness.
[To be married.]

She blushed like a rose.

To see Yankee girls is good
for sore eyes.

Like a girl's mind, no two minutes alike.

He tried to soft soap her.
[To flatter.]

She is as sweet as maple sugar.

Shining like a girl's face when she is
a fixing to be married.

She has a heart as big as a house.
[Very kind.]

As happy as two love birds.

As pretty as a goggle-eyed perch.

She sets her cap for him.
[Trying to win affection.]

To look pretty enough to tempt a fellow
to bite a piece out of her.

As pleased as a young couple at their
first christening.

Girls as sweet as full-blown roses.

Her lips looked like two red raspberries
just going to drop off from their bushes.

She's as beautiful as a day in spring.

As lovely as a prom queen.

He gave her as many kisses as would
cover a barn door.

She has no more sense than to put a
milk bucket under a bull.

IGNORANCE
— AND —
INAPTITUDE

He is so stupid that if you put his brain
in a bird it would fly backwards.

To have a dearth of corn in the attic.
[To lack brains.]

She doesn't know enough to
blow on hot soup.

He is a real chowder-head.
[Stupid.]

He hasn't got a brain in his body nor
any place to put one.

To have bats in the belfry.

Not to know enough to pound sand
into a rat-hole.

If brains were manure, you wouldn't
have enough to grow grass
out of your ears.

To have one's head full of cobwebs.

As stupid as an oyster.

He hasn't got all his buttons.

You wouldn't know beans if the
bag were untied.

He can't walk and chew tobacco
at the same time.

To be a saphead.

He is so stupid he couldn't roll rocks
down a steep hill.

Not to know one's ear from one's elbow.

She has no more sense than to put a
milk bucket under a bull.

To have nobody home in
the upper story.

He don't know nothing and always will.

She is so stupid that she is unable to boil
water without burning it.

He doesn't know enough to warm his
feet when they're cold.

If brains were dynamite, you wouldn't
have enough to blow your nose.

He doesn't know enough to pour water
out of a boot with the directions
written on the heel.

She doesn't have as many brains
as an oyster.

To be a regular dough-head.

To be unable to tell chalk from cheese.

As free of brains as a frog is
free of feathers.

You would hold a fish under water
to drown it.

She doesn't know how many
beans make five.

He hasn't got the brains
God gave geese.

Not to know enough to ache when
one is in pain.

He doesn't have sense enough to
carry guts to a bear.

As big as a whale.

SIZES
AND
SHAPES

No bigger than a pint of cider.

Shaped like an old apple tree.

As straight as a loon's leg.

So short he'd have to stand on a bucket
to look down a woodchuck hole.

Flatter than a flounder.

As snug as a pea in its pod.

Big as life and twice as natural.

He was squeezed as flat as a pancake.

As big as a whale.

Empty and hollow as a nutshell.

As square as a block of granite.

He's so thin he has to stand twice in the
same place to make a good shadow.

Not big enough to swing a cat
around by its tail.

As tall as a haypole.

The hills are so steep that chickens
lay square eggs so they won't roll
out of the nest.

As small as a bee's knee.

To be knocked into a cocked hat.
[Knocked out of shape.]

She is so thin you have to shake the
sheets to find her.

He's a great gawking gander.

As big as a church steeple.

As snug as a bird's nest.

To stand knee high to a grasshopper.
[Not very tall.]

Breasts as big as melons.

Skinnier than a bar of soap after
a hard day's wash.

As straight as a ramrod.
[Erect.]

His pigs are so lean it takes two of them
to make a shadow.

To be six feet and seven axe handles.
[Very tall person.]

As big as all outdoors.

No bigger than a fly's ear.

Happier than a pig in a puddle of mud.

COMPARISONS
— WITH —
THAN

Tougher than a catamount.

Bigger than a barn.
[Huge.]

Something being rarer than
a three-legged calf.

Happier than a pig in a puddle of mud.

Tighter than the shingles on a roof.

This is slower than death boiled
down and sugared off.

Stiller than last year's bird's nest.

He is fatter than the rear end of
a horse going west.

She doesn't need this any more than
a hen needs teeth.

Blacker than a black cat's belly.

Higher than a fairground fence.

To be thicker than two hands
in a mitten.
[To be good friends.]

He is crazier than a woodpecker
drumming on a tin chimney.

To be slicker than a four-inch trout.

She is thinner than a hayrake.

He is homelier than a basket
of knot-holes.

Fatter than a settled minister.

To know no more than a hog does
about a holiday.

Quieter than a mouse peeing on
a cotton ball.

His mood is lower than a mole's belly
button that's been digging all day.

You are meaner than goose grease.

Darker than a stack of black cats with
their eyes put out.

He has no more backbone than an eel.

Faster than a lovesick sailor on
a three-hour pass.

It's been drier than a covered bridge.

Easier than peeling a hard-boiled egg.

He doesn't need it any more than
a toad needs a watch.

Hotter than hell's back-kitchen.

DILIGENCE
AND
LAZINESS

He's a good old dog but he doesn't
like to hunt.

To put one's hand to the plow.

Busy as the devil in a gale of wind.

She's too lazy to ache when
she is in pain.

To paddle one's own canoe.

We have worked like sailors, and we
can eat like them.

He is so lazy he stops plowing to fart.

To do something right up to the handle.
[Very skillfully.]

To be idle as a painted ship upon a
painted ocean.

She worked her fingers to the bone.

He was born in the middle of the week
and looks both ways for Sunday.

Busy as a fiddler's elbow.

To be up before the crow puts
its shoes on.

He is so lazy he married a
pregnant woman.

To make short work of it.

Let them skin their own skunks.

To hang up one's fiddle.
[No more labor.]

As busy as a bee in a tar-barrel.

He worked double tides.

She doesn't have a lazy bone in her.

As busy as a cranberry merchant.

To grind one's own bait.

He worked like a farmhand at harvest.

About as active as a leftover
fly in January.

As lifeless as a string of dead fish.

Busy as twenty tailors around
a buttonhole.

He worked like the devil for his pay.

To wet neither foot nor finger
for something.
[To obtain without effort.]

As nervous as a long-tailed cat in a room full of rocking chairs.

CARES
— AND —
WORRIES

To be careful as a cat walking
on egg shells.

He was frightened out of
a year's growth.

To feel like a boiled owl.
[Nervously exhausted.]

You might as well kill me as scare
me to death.

As nervous as a long-tailed cat in a
room full of rocking chairs.

Not to care a chew of tobacco.

To be at the end of one's tether.

To fret in one's grease.

Not to be born in the woods to be
scared by an owl.

She doesn't give a straw.

He hasn't got the guts of a sparrow.

To stick out like a bump on a log.

Not to care a pin's head.

She was all curled up like
a burnt boot.

To crawl into a hole and pull the hole
in after you.

Helpless as spilled beans on a dresser.

To dread someone as a cat
hates hot soap.

As awkward as a wrong boot.

I'm as easy as an old glove, but a glove
ain't an old shoe to be trod on.

Not care a fiddlestick.

As jealous as a hen with young chickens.

To be struck all in a heap.
[Entirely overcome.]

To look at someone as pitiful as
a rabbit in a trap.

As melancholy as mice in
an empty mill.

He is as sensitive as a skinned eel.

To feel like a stewed witch.
[Tired.]

As helpless as a calf in a butcher's cart.

Fussing about like an old hen that's got
ducks for chickens.

To feel as low as a whale's belly.

To have cabin fever.

You might as well eat the devil as
sip his broth.

To be spineless as a jelly-fish.

He's scared skinny.

I'm so hungry I could eat the north end
out of a southbound skunk.

She's so nosy she can hear
the grass grow.

To feel like sinking down
in one's boots.

He has the guts of a butterfly.

Not to care a dried-apple damn.

I would not trust him as far as I could throw a bull by the tail.

LIES
AND
DECEPTIONS

To turn like a weathercock.

He lies as fast as a horse can trot.

So crooked he could hide behind a cork-screw.

I would not trust him as far as I could throw a bull by the tail.

To milk the town dry.
[To exploit.]

To be crooked as a hound's hind leg.

You'd take a worm from a blind
hen's mouth.

Not trust someone an inch beyond
one's nose.

She lies faster than water can
run down hill.

He let the cat out of the bag.

He's as straight as a yard of pump-water.

To take someone for a sleighride.
[To deceive someone.]

As sly as a fox when he is going
to rob a hen-roost.

There is a snake in the grass.

He would steal the tobacco out of
your mouth if you yawned.

To sail under false colors.

To pull the wool over someone's eyes.

That's a lie out of the whole cloth.
[An utter falsehood.]

He puts on more airs than
a country studhorse.

He lies so much that his wife has to
call the dog for him.

To catch a weasel asleep.

About as secretive as a cricket.

Sneaky as a sheep-killing dog.

He feels as big as a meeting house.
[Overly important.]

As crooked as a cow's horn.

She bought a pig in a poke.

They bend the way the wind blows.

You can trust him as far as you can
throw a meeting house by the steeple.

Short and sweet, like a donkey's gallop.

TIME
— AND —
SPACE

It's only a squirrel's jump away.

Quicker than hell could scorch
a feather.

He is so far behind he thinks
he is in front.

Within two rows of apple-trees.
[Moderate distance.]

Longer than a wet week.

As long as the rivers run.

He lives so far back in the hills that a
groundhog has to carry the mail.

It's so old it came out of Noah's
ark on crutches.

Many an applecart will tip over
before then.

He is just about between hay and grass.
[Between man- and boyhood.]

To be longer than a brook.

It is just a few hoe handles
down the road.

This place is so dead that it makes a
morgue look like a merry-go-round.

To have to wait until the
cows come home.
[A long time.]

Older than the devil's grandfather.

Short and sweet, like a donkey's gallop.

The room is so empty that there isn't a
peg to hang a thought on.

To steal a minute between the tide
and the eddy.

To be packed as closely as sardines
in a box.

It's so crowded here you have to go
outside to change your mind.

Up the road a hoot and a holler.
[Short distance.]

To be too old a bird to learn
a new tune.

I haven't seen you in a dog's age.
[Long time.]

When robins wear overalls.
[Never.]

Not to come within forty rows
of apple trees.
[Very far off.]

Like shooting fish in a barrel.

FISH
AND
WATER

As red as a lobster.

To sail close to the wind.

So stupid as to be unable to find salt
water in the sea.

As happy as a clam on Cape Cod beach.

To nail one's colors to the masthead.

Not worth an oyster-shell.

Easy as shooting fish in a barrel.

To keep an eye to windward.

As white as ocean foam.

To be out of one's depth.

No more than a sprat in a whale's belly.

To sail against wind and tide.

He is as dumb as codfish.

As unstable as the waves.

All mingled, mixed, and conglomerated
like a Connecticut chowder.

As pale as a soft-shelled clam.

The sail was as stiff as sheet-iron.

To squirm like eels in a basket.

Saltier than the briny ocean.

To be ship-shape.
[In good order.]

Happy as a clam in the mud.

She doesn't need that any more than
the sea needs water.

To be on one's own hook.
[On one's own.]

He feels as strong as the mainmast.

Tough as a Cape Cod fisherman.

Calm as the summer sea.

To take the wind out of someone's sails.

As hungry as a shark.

Not the only pebble on the beach.

It's raining pitchforks and barnshovels.

CLIMATE
— AND —
TEMPERATURE

To rain pitchforks with saw logs
for handles.

Fog as thick as pea soup.

As hot as a July bride in a feather bed.

It's cold enough to freeze the hair
off a dog's back.

To come forward like frogs after
a heavy rain.

It is as hot as mink in this room.

It's blowing great guns.
[To blow a gale.]

It was hot enough to melt the nose
off a brass monkey.

The fog is so thick you can hardly spit.

As white as a snow-bank.

Hardly enough rain to drown a flea.

Poor man's manure.
[Snow.]

Hot enough to fry one's brain
in one's skull.

He melted like snow in a June shower.

As fickle as the wind.

Hot as an iron pump handle on
a July noon.

As cold as a lamb's tail in
the January thaw.

It was so dry that the fish kicked up an awful dust getting upstream.

Hotter than hell's half-acre.

As cold as a gravestone in January.

As white as hoar frost.

It rained so hard that the water stood ten feet out of the well.

Colder than a dead puppy's nose.

As hot as love in hay time.

It's raining pitchforks and barn shovels.

It was cold enough to freeze two dry rags together.

To vanish like the morning dew.

As welcome as snow in harvest time.

It's so cold you have to milk the cows with wire pliers.

As fat as a woodchuck.

COMPARISONS
—WITH—
AS

Independent as a hog on ice.

As dull as a stockfish.

As cold as marble.

As slick as a hot knife through butter.

As sturdy as an oak.

As tough as a knot.

As plain as the way to market.
[Obvious.]

As sweet as new-mown hay.

As wet as a drowned rat.

As green as a watermelon.

As plenty as ditch-water.

As awkward as a cow with
a wooden leg.

As cheap as dog's meat.

As clean as a New England kitchen.

As sour as an old crab.

As sure as hell is a mousetrap.

As common as sawdust around
a sawmill.

As dumb as a man who can't find his
butt with a stick and a map.

As scarce as horse manure in
a two-car garage.

As rotten as an old stump.

As different as a whale and a tadpole.

As straight as a moose's course.

As calm as a millpond.

As plenty as herrings.

As naked as a peeled apple.

As welcome as water in a leaking ship.

As dumb as a stone wall.

As rotten as a three-day-old dead fish.

As sweet as syrup.

As gloomy as a graveyard on
a wet Sunday.

As black as a minister's coat.

As suspicious as a hairpin in
a bachelor's bed.

As fat as a woodchuck.

As yellow as a buttercup.

As empty as a gutted fish.

As steady as an old plow horse.

As painful as a slap in the belly
with a wet fish.

As unlikely as a mouse falling in
love with a cat.

As strong as a moose.

As hard as finding a pin's head in
a carload of hay.

As wise as a wisdom tooth.

As rare as a sailor on horseback.